A Caregiver's Journey

Rev. Rosa J. Caraballo

SOWING HOPE
BOOKS

A Caregiver's Journey

© 2021 Rev. Rosa J. Caraballo

Cover art by Michelle Martinez

Printed in the United States of America

ISBN-13: 978-1-7359627-7-1
LCCN: 2021900683

Sowing Hope Books
Tampa, Florida

Dedication

This is my legacy to my daughters, Ruth Deborah Caraballo, Tirzah Diane Caraballo; and to my grandchildren, Kaleb Hermes Smalls and Phoenix Rosa Smalls.

"You have surrounded me on every side, behind me and before me, and you have placed your hand gently on my shoulder." Psalm 135:5 (Voice Translation)

"The Lord bless you and keep you; the Lord make his face to shine upon you and be gracious to you; the Lord lift his countenance upon you and give you peace." Numbers 6:24-26 (ESV)

In memory of Rev. Dr. Hermes M. Caraballo, my husband, father to our daughters and spiritual encourager who deeply cared for the well-being of all who walked beside him.

Ubi caritas et amor, Deus ibi est.

Where charity and love are, there God is.

Acknowledgements

I would like to thank everyone who walked with me through this journey. You know who you are and everything you did along the way.

Thank you to the team at Publify for the guidance you provided in turning these words into a printed book I can share with others.

Contents

Dedication .... *i*

Acknowledgements..*ii*

Forward ....*iv*

Endorsements from Readers .... *v*

Chapter 1: *Journey With My Sustainer*........*1*

Chapter 2: *Caring for the Caregivers* *17*

Chapter 3: *Ministry of Presence* *37*

Chapter 4: *Memories of Healing and Loss*.. *51*

Chapter 5:*Sowing Hope* *65*

Chapter 6*: Caring for Souls* *85*

Chapter 7: *Transitions* *99*

Resources *117*

Forward

We have always been concerned about the lack of written historicity of the redemptive activity of God, left for us by the spiritual mothers and fathers of the Bronx, New York. Many have slipped into eternity, leaving no documentation of the past half century, especially as it pertains to the phenomenon of the caregiver, that secluded and mainly sequestered ministry with an audience of one. Rev. Rosa has brought an end to this drought. Our impoverished literary state is over with "A Caregiver's Journey." We know of no greater authority on the subject matter. However, there is no haughty expertise in these pages. This woman communicates from a grace-soaked place of experience. She is one of us.

Rev. Joseph & Melissa Cortese

Senior Pastors Crossroads Tabernacle
Bronx, New York

Endorsements from Readers

Rev. Rosa Caraballo, founder of Bruised Reed Ministry, was one of the most significant pioneer practitioners and powerful voices in the fight against AIDS, provided care and guidance to thousands in our New York City and beyond. She has decades of experience of providing Pastoral Care to those were afflicted with HIV/AIDS, her qualifications are impeccable. I still remember her annual Memorial Services to honor those that died of AIDS, and to help their families mourn and grieve their loved ones. Some of those services were held at the Latino Pastoral Action Center Urban Ministry Complex located in Bronx, New York. She is not only a compassionate caregiver but a fierce advocate for holistic care. She was the first Latina Palliative Care Chaplain at Montefiore Hospital in the Bronx.

In peace and freedom,

Bishop Raymond Rivera
Council of Holistic Christian Churches
and Ministry

"Reverend Rosa Caraballo sweeps you up and takes you along on her incredible journey of love, healing, and compassion. Telling stories that are both intimate and personal, she has traveled an inspiring path for over sixty years. Her generous sharing of the journey is poignant and remarkable. We learn about love, life, and death. Moreover, we learn how someone who faced great adversity throughout her life was able to sow hope. Thank you, Reverend Rosa, for your authentic voice. I am privileged and honored to have read your moving and beautiful journey - one that has many more chapters ahead.

Randi Kaplan LMSW

Director, Caregiver Support Center

Montefiore Medical Center,
Bronx, New York

Rev. Rosa Caraballo is a Woman of God who embodies Christ love for us as a Christian leader. She serves her Savior Jesus Christ sacrificially by serving those most in need because of terminal illness and health issues, sometimes who were hidden and forgotten. Rev Rosa while taking care of the least of these also taught us how to live our best life, full of joy and peace while serving. She's a true hero, teacher, mentor, pastor, author, and spiritual mother, who modeled for us what being a new creation in Christ could look like and feel like regardless of who we were and what had happened to us in life. I am forever grateful to her as a Mentor and Spiritual Mother.

Rev. Susana Rivera Leon

Executive Pastor, The Sanctuary Church
CEO Latino Pastoral Action Center, Bronx, New York

Chapter 1

Journey With My Sustainer

"Life's most urgent question is: What are you doing for others? We cannot all do great things, but we can do small things with great love. Be faithful in small things, because it is in them that your strength lies." **Mother Theresa**

"And because God is the source and sustainer of everything, everything finds fulfillment in him. May all praise and honor be given to him forever! Amen!"
Romans 11:36 (TPT)

So how does a woman from San Juan, Puerto Rico, who moved to Little Rock, Arkansas; Fayetteville, North Carolina; and to the Bronx, New York embrace a journey of caregiver? I invite you to join me as I document this journey of becoming a person who "walks alongside" people, offering hope.

As a Latina woman, I identify culturally as Boricua (colloquium derived from the land of Borinqueños one of the indigenous tribes of Puerto Rico) and as a grassroots activist. When these two identities collided with my spiritual life during my college years, I found myself full of discontent. I thought I had to choose between social activism and spirituality. Until one day, when I was encouraged to attend a meeting of InterVarsity Christian Fellowship by one of their campus leaders at Hunter College, NYC.

She said they were conducting a bible study on Jesus the Revolutionary. This was especially intriguing since, during that time-period of the 1970's, the Black Panthers and Young Lords were the known revolutionaries in our communities of color. The room was filled with students from all different cultural backgrounds. The emphasis was on how Jesus walked among the people, lived in the community, spoke out against injustices, and even allowed women to be part of this movement.

Matthew 9: 35-38 (ESV), "And Jesus went throughout all the cities and villages, teaching, in their synagogues and proclaiming the gospel of the kingdom and healing every disease and every affliction. When he saw the crowds, he had compassion for them, because they were harassed and helpless, like sheep without a shepherd. Then he said to his disciples, "the harvest is plentiful, but the laborers are few; therefore, pray earnestly to the Lord of the harvest to send out laborers into his harvest." These words of scripture are revolutionary.

My thinking soon shifted from Latino activists back to Christ. As time went on, I learned to incorporate my social, grassroots activism into my faith.

During my junior year of college, I worked as a part-time teller in a Citibank, located on the west side of Manhattan. Unbeknownst to me at that time, the staff of InterVarsity lived a few blocks away. I was outside on my break when I ran into Barbara from InterVarsity. Coincidence? Barbara told me about a yearly Discipleship training being held that summer and encouraged me to attend. So, I went to Gordon College, in Wenham, Massachusetts to attend the training. It was a life changing experience.

Barbara gave me a book on Jonah. He was a man in the Bible who received a calling to go to the city of Nineveh to preach. Instead of answering the call, Jonah ran away. While on a ship, a storm arose. Jonah told the shipmates the storm was occurring because he was running away from the Presence of God. They tossed him into the sea, and he cried out to the Lord in distress. Then, God allowed him to survive. He got to Nineveh and gave the people the message God had for them. And, they came to believe in God. Inside this book Barbara inscribed, "You are running from your call to missions in New York City. Maybe this story will inspire you". You see, God's love was so great for the people of Nineveh that he sent Jonah. And now, he was calling me to show his love and care for others. "The Sovereign LORD has given me his words of wisdom, so that I know how to comfort the weary. Morning by morning he wakens me and opens my understanding to his will." Isaiah 50:4 (NLT)

I still struggled with the calling.

My parents had retired during my sophomore year in college and moved to Puerto Rico. My sister, Rachel, and I remained in New York to finish our studies. We lived with the Gonzalez family who attended the church where I grew up. Their daughter, Eva, and I have been friends since we were five years old and remain sister-friends to this day. In 1977, I completed my studies at Hunter College, attaining a BA in Sociology and minor in Puerto Rican Studies. As a graduation present, my parents sent me a one-way ticket to Puerto Rico (they were trying to convince me to stay and work in PR). We had a great time together, traveling around the entire island. Researching for work on the island led me to find out that social workers in Puerto Rico at that time received a very small salary.

One day I received a phone call from a dear friend, asking if I'd please come back to New York. Her sister and husband were struggling with heroin addiction and they needed help. There were several faith-based substance abuse programs in New York City that I was familiar with. I could have told her about the programs but, because I still hadn't found work in Puerto Rico, I took this as a sign to go back to the United States. When I returned to the Bronx, I was able to get them into programs for substance abuse; her sister into *New Life for Girls* (NLFG) and her husband into *Teen Challenge*. Their children were also placed in programs for children with special needs.

I thought, "Lord isn't that enough?" No! God had other plans. The directors of NLFG asked me if I could volunteer, while I was searching for a job, so I said, "Yes." The women in the program and staff were praying that the Lord would lead me to work there and be a missionary in the NLFG ministry. One Sunday, while in church, as I went up for prayer, an elder, who knew nothing of my internal struggle, said these words: "Rosa, God is calling you to missions and it isn't far away. It's here in the city!" As I proceeded to my usual seat in church, the group from NLFG was entering church! Well, I knew God was orchestrating something when my pastor, the late Bishop Gerald Kaufman, preached on Jonah in Nineveh!

That night was a restless night. I kept telling the Lord I wanted to work and make money and have two apartments, one in New

York and the other in Puerto Rico, and I knew that wouldn't be possible as a missionary!

"It is not the healthy who need a doctor, but the sick…"
Matthew 9:12 (NIV).

God won!

Most of my family members were supportive. My mother and some of my close friends, however, were in shock. They couldn't believe that I, "the radical/activist," was going into full-time ministry. Eventually, they all accepted my calling! My church family and friends were very supportive. Before I knew it, I was in Dover, Pennsylvania in staff training at NLFG Ministries. And, soon after that, I became Dean of Women at their NLFG Center in Bayamon, Puerto Rico. God kept me bi-coastal; he gave me the desire of my heart in a different way!

Two years later, when I got married to Rev. Hermes M. Caraballo that was also orchestrated by God. (By the way, Rev. Caraballo had also come to work at NLFG, after he'd previously worked with Teen

Challenge in New York and then served as youth pastor at a church in Tampa, Florida.) I was now under another type of calling, to minister wherever we were called. Guess where? My Nineveh, the Bronx, New York. So, for 13 years, we served as pastors at Glad Tidings Church in Bronx, New York. We served the community with holistic hospital, prison, and homeless ministries. In addition to those, we also ran a food pantry for the community. After pastoring at Glad Tidings, we moved on to become pastors at Grace Tabernacle, also located in Bronx, New York. We pastored there for eight years, until 2004.

In 1984, while pregnant with our youngest daughter, I read an article in the New York Times on "Border Babies." These were babies left abandoned in the hospital, because they had AIDS! My heart leaped when my inner voice said, "You need to do something about this situation." Soon after, my husband was preaching a series from Isaiah 42:3 (NIV), "a bruised reed he shall not break…in faithfulness he will bring forth justice." During this series, the Lord spoke to my husband, telling him to start a ministry for people who were "bruised reeds," people with AIDS. God told my husband, "You are to separate Rosa for this ministry." When they were told the vision, the church stood up in total support!

"Take the first step in faith. You don't have to see the whole staircase, just take the first step".
Dr. Martin Luther King Jr.

In 1985, I took my step into the HIV/AIDS pandemic. Back then, HIV/AIDS carried a huge stigma. People often treated those with HIV/AIDS as if they were lepers. No one wanted to be around them for fear of contracting the disease. Most communities of faith had great difficulty in ministering to those afflicted and affected by HIV/AIDS. They didn't see this epidemic as a ministry they should have separated for "missionaries or lay leaders."

In 1991, our local church and advisory board felt that I should be licensed as a minister. So, my credentialing as a minister came from another body, Harvest International Fellowship (HIF), which was led by one of my mentors in ministry, the late Bishop G. Randolph Gurley. Dr. Gurley encouraged me to get a Master's Degree in Theology, with emphasis on Pastoral Care and Counseling from Vision Christian University. My ordination service came in 1993. HIF recognized a person's gifting is important, as I wasn't called to the pastorate, and I am not a preacher either. They saw that God had merged my secular education (social work) with my spiritual gifts (teaching, exhorting), thus giving me the desire of ministering to "those people who many wouldn't touch." Or, as I once heard a spiritual leader describe people living with HIV/AIDS as being, "modern day lepers." My calling was all about being present, caring and offering hope to persons afflicted and affected by HIV/AIDS. Listening is an important skillset for ministry. Listen to God. Listen to His people.

Although it took many years for some of the faith community and colleagues in ministry to accept this calling, the people afflicted and affected by HIV/AIDS, along with AIDS Service organizations and the medical community, embraced me whole heartedly! This journey helped me to understand how important it is for the local and global church to be holistic and compassionate. They need to reach out into their surroundings – the community and its residents, ensuring they are addressing the physical, intellectual, emotional, social and spiritual needs of the people in the community at large, not just of those within the household of faith.

The local and global church should be a place of refuge, while providing nurturing and support, as well as being a restorative community of healing for the body, mind and soul. This aspect has been the guiding force for ministry to those that are afflicted. Seneca, of ancient Rome, asked, "Who is there in all the world who listens to us? Here I am, this is me in my nakedness, with my wounds, my secret grief, my despair, my betrayal, my pain, which I can't express, my terror, my abandonment. Oh, listen to me for a day, an hour, a moment, lest I expire in my terrible wilderness, my lonely silence. Oh God, is there no one who will listen?"

My vision of local and global holistic ministry started with the passage in Isaiah 61:1,2,8,(NLT), "The Spirit of the Sovereign Lord is upon me, for the Lord has anointed me to bring the good news to the poor. He has sent me to comfort the brokenhearted and to proclaim that captives will be released, and prisoners will be freed. He has sent me to tell those who mourn that the time of the Lord's favor has come... For I, the Lord, love justice. I hate robbery and wrongdoing. I will faithfully reward my people for their suffering and make an everlasting covenant with them."

These scriptures establish the foundation for compassionate ministry. I believe that as God has made a covenant with us, bound Himself to fulfill his purpose on earth through men and women, so I have taken on the challenge to sow hope into the lives of those afflicted and affected by HIV/AIDS. Several passages of scripture guide this process such as Psalm 41:1-3 (NLT), "Oh, the joys of those who are kind to the poor! The Lord rescues them when they are in trouble. The Lord protects them and keeps them alive. He gives them prosperity in the land and rescues them from their enemies. The Lord nurses them when they are sick and restores them to health." We gain another biblical response regarding care of the soul and ministry to the sick and dying.

This call has pursued me by way of Psalm 69:20,29 (ESV), "Reproaches have broken my heart, so that I am in despair. I looked for pity, but there was none, and for comforters, but I found none...But I am afflicted and in pain; let your salvation, O God, set me on high!"

For the past many years, the scriptures that have sustained me are in Psalm 73:25,26 (ESV), "Whom have I in heaven but you? And there is nothing on earth that I desire beside you. My flesh and my heart fail, but God is the strength of my heart and my portion forever."

The HIV/AIDS pandemic is one of the significant issues that impacted my life and my family. It enhanced the way I do ministry. My heart has been enlarged in this journey of sowing hope to those afflicted, affected and abandoned because of HIV/AIDS. Truthfully, at times, it has been a lonely journey because many people in ministry didn't want to embrace *Persons Living With HIV/AIDS* (PLWHA's) and resented my advocacy on their behalf. As my editor and publisher stated in the forward of my book, *Covenant of Hope, Pacto de Esperanza,* "...she became the person she is today: The church girl who grew up to be an AIDS activist."

Most of my context of ministry has been in the areas of holistic local church experience; substance abuse and recovery. *Bruised Reed Ministry* (BRM) was an HIV/AIDS para-church ministry that grew into one of the first faith-based HIV/AIDS non-profit organizations in the South Bronx. These are also my strong ministry skill sets. Because of my desire to pursue hospital chaplaincy, I enrolled in the *Clinical Pastoral Education (CPE) Program* in Harlem Hospital to gain knowledge and experiences in other areas such as labor and delivery, pediatrics and general surgery, and enhance my ability to provide spiritual care in all environments. The chaplaincy and pastoral care would increase my opportunities for ministry and occupational goals of being a full-time chaplain in either palliative and/or end of life care.

In a course I took titled, "Personal Professional Theological Foundations of Ministry at Alliance Theological Seminary," Dr. Barbara E. Austin-Lucas told me, "Your gifts will make room for you. My prayer is that this next level of ministry will embrace all your gifts, skills and talent."

Jeremiah 29:11 (NIV) *says, "For I know the plans I have for you declares the Lord. Plans to prosper you and not to harm you. Plans to give hope and a future."*

Psalm 54:4 (Berean Study Bible) says, "Surely God is my helper; the Lord is the sustainer of my soul."

As you continue this journey with me, my prayer is that you see God's heart and the purpose He has for you. See his ability to pursue us in the journey, equipping us, supplying for our needs, and sustaining us through all the issues of life!

Chapter 2

Caring for the Caregivers

"There are only four kinds of people in this world: Those who have been caregivers; Those who currently are caregivers; Those who will be caregivers; and Those who will need caregivers."
Rosalyn Carter

According to **CAREGIVING IN THE U.S. 2020 Report, by** The *National Alliance for Caregiving* (NAC) and AARP, compared to 2015 (43.5 million), a greater proportion of caregivers of adults are providing care to multiple people now, with 24 percent caring for two or more recipients (up from 18 percent in 2015). In 2020, the totals have grown to 53 million. Among today's caregivers who are caring for family members, 39% are men and 61% are women. These findings, in combination with the increased prevalence of caregiving, suggest a nation of Americans who continue to step up to help provide unpaid care to family, friends, and neighbors who might need assistance due to health or functional needs.

The Family Caregiver Alliance definition: A **caregiver** – sometimes called an *informal caregiver* – is an unpaid individual (for example, a spouse, partner, family member, friend, or neighbor) involved in assisting others with activities of daily living and/or medical tasks. *Formal caregivers* are paid care providers, who are giving care in one's home or in a care setting (day care, residential facility, or long-term care facility). As for the purposes of the present fact sheet, displayed statistics generally refer to caregivers of adults. Approximately 43.5 million caregivers have provided unpaid care to an adult or child in the last 12 months. [National Alliance for Caregiving and AARP, (2015). *Caregiving in the U.S.*] About 15.7 million adult family caregivers care for someone who has Alzheimer's disease or other dementia. [Alzheimer's Association, 2015). *2015 Alzheimer's Disease Facts and Figures.*] In 2000, the National Family Caregiver Support program was established to fund support for informal caregivers to care for their loved ones at home.

In 2011, Montefiore Medical Center opened the first Caregiver Support Center (The Arthur D. Emil Caregiver Support Center), directed by Randi L. Kaplan, LMSW, and located at the Moses campus. Then in 2014, the second one was opened at the Jack D. Weiler campus, led by Julie List, LMSW. These sites provide a calming environment for the family of patients and caregivers, to help them relax, as well as receiving the support of a social worker or trained volunteer. When I was the Palliative Care Chaplain at Montefiore, these centers became a vital resource for our teams, located at both campuses. The one located at the Moses Campus was directly next to the Interfaith Chapel, which enabled us to also help when caregivers experienced spiritual distress.

> *"Every believer has received grace gifts, so use them to serve one another, as faithful stewards of the many-colored tapestry of God's grace."* **1 Peter 4:10** *(TPT)*

Caregiving for The Sick:

Since the creation, God ordained caregiving to the earth, and all its creatures and then to people. We are called to have a compassionate response, and to protect and restore the needs of human beings. Love and Faith is our connection to God and each other – Pain and Hope is what we share on this journey. Caregivers face the pressures of daily life. They are squeezed physically, mentally, emotionally and spiritually. Life as they knew it is dramatically changed. Transitioning from a job and career, to be a stay at home caregiver, creates an enormous amount of stress for many families. Illness forces us to rearrange our life, our work schedules, our home environment, and our social life. It also affects our finances and mental state of health, as the intensity and types of care can vary from day to day.

I experienced it all and learned that to be an effective caregiver one must be able to:

- Confront the challenges that arise
- Ask for help or seek support
- Utilize resources available

Our body and soul carry this burden, however as we read in Hebrews 4:16 (NLT), "So let us come boldly to the throne of our gracious God. There we will receive his mercy, and we will find grace to help us when we need it most. Grace strengthens and will make you whole!"

For me, caregiving took on a different light in an expanded context in 1985, when Bruised Reed Ministry commenced as a para-church ministry of Glad Tidings Church in the Bronx, New York. Then, in 1995, as executive director, we transitioned to become a faith-based HIV/AIDS, 501c3, non-profit organization. To expand these services to people living with HIV/AIDS, we relocated into office space at the Latino Pastoral Action Center. We applied for, and received, grants from the New York Woman's Foundation, The Sister Fund, The New York Foundation, Union Square Award and Esperanza, US. These grants helped develop support programs for people living with HIV/AIDS. Some were widows. All were caregivers. The following scripture guided me in this ministry. Romans 15:13 (NLT) says, "I pray that God, the source of hope, will fill you completely with joy and peace because you trust in him. Then you will overflow with confident hope through the power of the Holy Spirit." My mission was to sow hope in the lives of people afflicted and affected by HIV/AIDS.

- We conducted educational seminars and support groups.
- Our Back to School project provided children with school supplies, while churches partnered with us to donate supplies and distribute them.
- Boxes of Love provided all the necessary groceries to make a Thanksgiving meal, which was taken directly to their home the prior weekend.
- Madre Positiva, an annual Mother's Day luncheon organized by our Covenant of Hope AIDS Taskforce, sought donations from small businesses. World Vision's

Storehouse donated gifts, which were all put into a gift bag that also included a small bottle of Alpha & Omega anointing oil.

- Candlelight & Healing Service conducted annually on Worlds AIDS Day (December 1), provided spiritual support to individuals, family and friends affected by the disease.
- Invited to conducted workshops and participate in panel discussions at various national HIV/AIDS conferences.

In 2002, my husband encouraged me to attend Alliance Theological Seminary. It totally enhanced my work as HIV Palliative Care chaplain, on a three-year, Health Resources Services Administration (HRSA) research grant to provide palliative care to patients with HIV/AIDS at Montefiore Medical Center and in the community.

It was important to continue educating people about HIV/AIDS and document the work of Bruised Reed Ministry. So, in 2004, with a grant from Nueva Esperanza's Hispanic Capacity Project and The Sister Fund, Ebed Press published our bilingual (English/Spanish) book, *Covenant of Hope,*

Pacto de Esperanza, A Woman's Healing Journey in the AIDS Epidemic. This book contained the personal stories written by women living with HIV/AIDs and served as an educational tool.

My husband, Hermes, was a bi-professional minister. He pastored Grace Tabernacle Church, served as director of Community Affairs at the Bronx Borough President Office, and was a leader of the Bronx Clergy Taskforce. On the morning of on September 27, 2004, as he got ready for work, I heard a loud bang, and a thump in the bathroom, which was right next to our bedroom. I ran to the bathroom, and opened the door, while trying to keep our dog Pookie from entering. There was Hermes, slumped in the tub with one hand hanging on the shower curtain. There are no words to accurately describe the surge of energy that was flowing through my body! He had a pulse and was breathing. But, he was unresponsive! Facts you should know: My husband was six feet tall and weighed more than 250 pounds. I am five feet, two inches tall! The space between the tub, cabinet, toilet and door was literally less than three feet. I lifted him out of the tub and onto the floor. But, then I couldn't open the door. So, I shifted him to the side. I called out to my daughters to call 911, and then managed to put some shorts on him. Ruth, Tirzah and I were wrought with emotions, and Pookie wouldn't stop whining. Our local Fire Department (FDNY) was the first to arrive. Emergency Medical Service (EMS) arrived right after that. After EMS evaluated him, they told us they'd take him to Jacobi Medical Center (located several miles away). We objected, because Montefiore Medical Center was exactly two blocks away and it was where his doctors were. EMS team was adamant. But, thank God for the intervention of FDNY captain, who knew my husband from his job with the Bronx Borough President's office. He told EMS they would personally take him to Montefiore. So, EMS agreed and took him to the emergency department of Montefiore.

The neurology doctor evaluated Hermes, gave him an injection of tissue plasminogen activator (tPA) used to treat ischemic stroke and he was transferred to the stroke unit at Montefiore Medical Center. He was totally unresponsive. During a family meeting the neurologist told us, "We are looking at imminent death – do you understand what that is?"

Hermes' cardiologist, "Dr. B.," was standing next to me and he said, "Rosa does, because she works in palliative care. But, it's probably the first time the rest of the family is hearing this."

The neurologist proceeded to further explain what they would look for in a three-day timeline. The question arose, "If there is no response after the third day?" DEATH!

My response to the doctors was, "If Hermes responds by the third day, then we are having a prayer service right here, to give God thanks for healing!"

His cardiologist smiled and told me that he didn't even go to synagogue!

That third day, as his brother, Louie (who flew in from Arizona), and I were at Hermes' bedside in the stroke unit, he suddenly opened his eyes, and said to Louie, "Bro,' what are you doing here? Then he turned to me and said, "Ro, I love you so much"! We cried tears of joy and the medical team immediately rushed over. The family was in the waiting room and we definitely praised God for his divine intervention!

Once Hermes was stabilized, he was transferred to a nursing home facility until he regained more strength. While he was there, visiting hours were more flexible than the stroke unit. One afternoon, Pastor David Serrano Sr. was at his bedside, spoon feeding him food that his wife prepared just for Hermes. He did this weekly during the time Hermes was in the nursing home. Other clergy, friends and family would alternate their visits to not overwhelm him while he recovered from the stroke.

After further progress, it was determined Hermes could be transferred to the Lubin Center, an Acute Inpatient Rehabilitation, located at Einstein Hospital in Bronx, New York, for a few months. Afterwards, he was discharged home to receive additional physical, occupational and speech therapy. He needed assistance with all his basic needs and couldn't walk on his own. This was one of the most traumatic events that changed my life and limited my ministry. I had to interrupt my seminary studies and eventually close Bruised Reed Ministry, because no one wanted to take on the responsibility of running the organization. I became Hermes' caregiver. Thankfully his mother, Isabel, and my youngest daughter, who still lived at home, helped to provide daily physical care as well. Being homebound because of his physical disabilities because of the stroke, Rev. Dr. Raymond Rivera and Bishop Ronald Bailey came often to our apartment to provide fellowship, as well as emotional and spiritual support. I am so grateful for my friends, Eva and Carmen, who would take me grocery shopping, while Iliana and Madeline would call and come by to check up on me and make me laugh!

After much rehabilitative therapy, Hermes recuperated nicely. In May of 2005, my nephew contacted us, because he wanted Hermes to officiate his wedding ceremony in Florida. All his doctors cleared him to fly to Sarasota, Florida. Our local New York Police Department (NYPD) community affairs gave us a special badge, so that we could board early. When we landed in Florida, Jet Blue's airline captain insisted she would wheel Hermes off the plane!

Hermes performed the wedding ceremony on May 28. It was a beautiful beach wedding, and all our families gathered to celebrate. The next day my daughters returned to New York for work and the rest of the family decided to have a family barbeque by the pool. They asked Hermes what he would like to eat, and he said, "A porterhouse steak", which my nieces' husband prepared for him. My grandnephews had a great time pushing him around in his wheelchair. We called it a day and went to our rooms in the hotel. Our friends, Pastor John and Diane Baschieri, were schedule to pick Hermes and I up to spend some time with them in Lehigh Acres, Florida. So, after putting Hermes in bed, I started to pack our luggage. Hermes said, "Ro, please come to bed."

But, I explained that I couldn't leave it all for the morning.

Again, he pleaded, "Please." I got into the bed and he said, "Please hold me tight."

A few hours later I heard the strange gurgling sound and noticed he was unresponsive. I called 911 and asked my family that were in the hotel to come to our room.

The ambulance arrived immediately and took us to Sarasota Memorial Hospital, which was literally a few blocks from the hotel. Hermes was taken to the stroke unit and the neurologist explained that the stroke had affected the other side of his brain and since we had advance directives, Do Not Resuscitate (DNR) and Do Not Intubate (DNI), the neurologist said he would move us to the hospice unit of the hospital. The doctor asked me what our occupations were, and I told him we were both ordained ministers and I was a chaplain. He then asked if he could pray with us! Once in the hospice unit, I called my daughters and they were distraught, because they couldn't fly back to Florida to be with us. Pastor John and Diane, along with their family came from Lehigh Acres, Florida to be with us at the hospital. They prayed and sang (Hermes was also a musician). Our daughters called family and former church friends that lived in New York and Florida to let them know what was happening. Jeanette Roman, daughter of Madeline Diaz (one of the young women who grew up in our former church, Glad Tidings) drove from Pinellas, Florida. When she arrived, she immediately asked me if I had eaten. I told her no, so she went and got me a turkey sandwich, because she knew what I liked. A few hours later, Hermes died of a hemorrhagic cerebral vascular stroke. I lost my husband – life and ministry partner Hermes Miguel Caraballo – when he died of a second stroke at Sarasota Memorial Hospital. I left Florida and returned to New York with a great hole in my soul. I have become a widow and God has become my Sustainer!

My daughters, Ruth and Tirzah, had made all the funeral arrangements. When I arrived back home at our apartment in New York, our dog Pookie was overjoyed with excitement, until he realized Hermes wasn't with me. He kept going back to the door with expectancy and leaped every time the doorbell rang, or someone knocked, again disappointed Hermes wasn't there. We were all heartbroken!

Hermes was a giver, so much so that the day after I got back from Florida, I received a phone call from the Director of Fox's Funeral Home, expressing his condolences, while proceeding to tell me that the purchased burial plots "we had," Hermes had given away! What??? Then he told me that he had negotiated with Kensico Cemetery to get two plots further over from the family plots at the same rate! God intervened immediately. Our dear friend, Pastor Mark Gorman, called me from Louisiana and said God told him to call me because I needed help. I told him what happened, and he posted on his website what we needed and said he would bring a check for the funeral when he arrived in New York. Bishop Bailey, from Love Gospel Assembly in the Bronx, New York, called. He also said he'd take a check to the funeral home to cover expenses. We laid Hermes to rest (down the block, as my girls said) from the gravesites of his father and brothers.

Pastor Mark Gorman, his ministry and my family provided some financial support for me to take a long-needed sabbatical. Isaiah 57:10 (NIV), "You wearied yourself by such going about, but you would not say 'it is hopeless. You found renewal of your strength, and so you would not faint." Well known minister and author, Bishop T. D. Jakes, writes in his book **Crushing** the following statement, "Everyone, however, must learn the value, healing qualities, and even necessity of being alone to rest, recharge, receive divine insight, and purge what has been affecting them."

After you've had your husband as your pastor for more than 20 years, seeking a new place to congregate becomes difficult. So many of the local pastors encouraged me to attend their churches, but I just stayed home. One weekend, my dear friends, Carmen and Iliana, told me they were picking me up to go to church with them. So, I went with them to Crossroads Tabernacle, the church founded by Pastor Aimee Cortese and now led by her son, Pastor Joseph Henry Cortese. There, I was reunited with people I knew. And, I met many new people. Shortly after, I met with the pastors and explained that I wanted to sit and heal from my grief and that I appreciated their support. I needed "different" in my life. I soon became a member of Crossroads Tabernacle. Eventually, pastors Joseph and Melissa Cortese asked me if I would lead a small group, "Sowing Hope," for persons affected and afflicted by HIV/AIDS, while utilizing my book, *Covenant of Hope*. Many years later, I conducted a few workshops for Caregivers at the church and to this day many of those involved remain in touch with me!

In 2007, I returned to Alliance Theological Seminary (ATS) to finish my Master's Degree, with concentration in Urban Ministry, and was able to graduate in 2009. During this time, I did some consulting work for World Vision N.Y. and served on the Board of Directors for Manna of Life Ministries (MOLM), which provides nourishment to those underserved and living in the food deserts of the Bronx, NY. Being actively involved with

MOLM gave me a sense of purpose and provided a community that was like-minded in service to persons afflicted and affected by different illnesses, and who suffered from food insecurity and lived, in food deserts (communities lacking fresh, healthy food). They even supported me with groceries, and a Metrocard (used for public transportation in New York), so that I could finish my Clinical Pastoral Education course at Harlem Hospital in NYC, which was required for chaplaincy work. Now the challenge became finding a chaplaincy position when, in 2009, we experienced an economic crisis. The following two years were very challenging, with being unemployed, since resources were scarce. Thankfully, my daughter, Tirzah, lived with me, and was working and took on many of the financial responsibilities. I am grateful to God for all the family and friends that were encouraging, financially supportive and helped with job searches. In 2011, gratefully, Dr. Peter Selwyn, Chairperson of the Department of Family and Social Medicine of Montefiore Hospital, secured a position for me as Chaplain for the Palliative Care Service, which I held until my retirement in 2018.

Lord,

We find ourselves in the season of life where illness has afflicted our loved one and affected our lives. Sometimes we are strong but many times we are fragile. I pray the you Lord replenish our souls and may the burden of our hearts be lightened. May our hope be restored by the encouragement we receive. Amen.

Chapter 3

Ministry of Presence

"Reweaving shalom means to sacrificially thread, lace, and press our time, power, goods and resources into the lives and needs of other." Timothy J. Keller

Most of my ministry life has been in the borough of the Bronx, New York, that currently has a population of 1.43 million. There is a great cultural diversity found in the Bronx, including African, Black/African American, Asian, Caribbean, European, Irish, Italian, Latino and many more. I have lived in the Southwest Bronx, Hunt's Point, Mott Haven (mostly known at the South Bronx) and in the Northwest section, Norwood. Bruised Reed Ministry was first started in the Northeast section at Glad Tidings Church and then in 1994 relocated to the South Bronx at the Latino Pastoral Action Center, until 2004.

We all need to receive guidance and be prepared for the open doors in the journey to be an agent of change in our communities and the world. Many people in spiritual leadership and/or ministry don't see that what they are doing is caregiving, caring for souls, and giving of themselves by speaking life into the lives of people. They are walking beside them and helping them in their journey of life. In the field of ministry life and chaplaincy, I had two women that lived this path and influenced me.

The first was Rev. Aimee Cortese, who I met as a young girl, when she was the only Pentecostal minister that frequently preached in the Third Spanish Baptist Church that I grew up in. Pastor Aimee, as we lovingly called her, was the first female chaplain in the history of the New York State Department of Corrections and served in the Bayview, Bedford Hills, Ossining, and Taconic Correctional Facilities. She was also one of the mentors of Latinas in Ministry and Founder of Crossroads Tabernacle, in Bronx, New York.

Ethel Bender also served as chaplain at Bedford Hills Correctional facility, and she served on the Board of New Life for Girls (which is how I met her). Ethel's husband, Rev. Martin Bender, pastored at Joy Fellowship, which was also in the Bronx, New York. These two women spoke into my life, taught me to lead with compassion, and walked beside me.

Being a chaplain in Palliative Care, one takes on the mission to help alleviate the spiritual distress, along with the pain that a patient, family member or staff is experiencing. I attended a health-care conference in Boston, Massachusetts and I heard Dr. Christina Puchalski say the following, "When you walk in the room, look into their eyes and fully connect to them. Really enjoy your interaction. Try to feel their anxiety or their happiness. Put your full attention onto him or her. It's your patient who may be feeling afraid, anxious, and in deep pain. You are this person's beacon of hope and of love. Think of yourselves as partners in the middle of an environment that may be very isolating. But, in the connection that both of you form, there is no isolation, and there is no fear. Instead, it is just love. It's love in the broadest sense of the word." This statement encompasses the ministry of presence or as I like to say, walk alongside someone, holistic ministry.

Spiritual Care must remain patient-centered. It requires us to be fully present, non-judgmental, and compassionate, while providing encouragement with realistic hope. It's all about providing a ministry of comfort and spiritual support for patients alienated from former religious/spiritual traditions. The patients' perspective on death and dying are usually dictated by their cultural and religious beliefs.

Montefiore Medical Center in the Bronx, New York is the academic medical center and University Hospital for Albert Einstein College of Medicine. It has several campuses throughout the Bronx and Westchester County, including a Children's Hospital, Medical Groups and Outpatient Clinics. My work in HIV Palliative Care chaplaincy started with the Department of Family and Social Medicine and years later as Palliative Care chaplain for the Moses and Weiler Campuses.

The World Health Organization (WHO) states, "Palliative medicine is the study and management of patients with active, progressive, and far-advanced disease for whom the prognosis is limited, and the focus of care is the quality of life. It is the active total care of patients whose disease is not responsive to curative treatment. Control of pain, along with other symptoms, and of psychological, social, and spiritual problems, is paramount. The goal of palliative care is achievement of the best quality of life for patients and their families."

The European Association for Palliative Care taskforce on Spiritual Care in Palliative Care 2010, defines Spirituality for Palliative Care Purposes: Spirituality is the dynamic dimension of human life that relates to the way persons (individuals and community) experience, express, and/or seek meaning, purpose, and transcendence and the way they connect, in the moment, to self, others, nature, the significant and or the sacred.

St. Augustine said, "You are to pay special attention to those who, by accidents of time, or place, or circumstances, are brought into closer connection with you." Palliative care is an approach that improves the quality of life for patients (adults and children) and their families who are facing problems associated with a life-threatening illness. It prevents and relieves suffering through the early identification, correct assessment and treatment of pain and other problems, whether physical, psychosocial or spiritual. Being a chaplain in Palliative Care is a mission to help alleviate their spiritual stress, pain, and offering healing prayers. We typically think of hope as a feeling that something desirable is likely to happen. Unlike a wish or longing, hope implies expectation of obtaining what is desired.

"Comfort and strength come from three powerful spiritual drugs: Faith, Hope and Love. My experience is that when combined with each other, they work synergistically and produce greater results. I hope by now you've had some moving experience that renewed your belief in Faith, Hope and Love. Experiencing these three spiritual realities can produce a deep feeling of well-being and purpose in life, along with feelings of comfort and strength." William Josef Dobbels. S.J.; *An Epistle of Comfort, Scriptural Meditations and Passages for Persons Suffering from AIDS.*

In Hebrew, *hope* is the word *tikvah* (teek-VAH). Strong's defines it as "a cord, expectation, and hope." It comes from the Hebrew root *kavah* meaning "to bind together, collect; to expect: – tarry, wait (for, on, upon)."

> *Colossians 1:28-29* (NLT), "So we tell others about Christ, warning everyone and teaching everyone with all the wisdom God has given us. We want to present them to God, perfect in their relationship to Christ. That's why I work and struggle so hard, depending on Christ's mighty power that works within me."

Charis – The word 'grace' (CHEN in Hebrew, CHARIS in Greek), as it is used in the scriptures, literally means 'favor,' 'to bend or stoop in kindness to another as a superior to an inferior.' It has the idea of graciousness in manner or action.

Being a "deep listening" presence.

Seeing the face of Christ in another.

Having the ability to connect with people.

Being available.

Empathy.

Expression of gracefulness in the healing power of attentive presence.

Allow that person to take you with them on their journey.

"No matter how sophisticated the technology of healing gets, true healing will involve three very simple human elements: compassion, touch, and conversation." Daniel P. Sulmasy, O.E. M., M.D., The Healers' Calling; He is a Franciscan friar and Assoc. Professor of Medicine, Director of the Center for Clinical Bioethics at Georgetown University Medical Center, Washington, DC

When I was a teenager, my sister, Raquel (who we call Rachel), taught me to crochet and I didn't know then what an impact it would have on my children, grandchildren, and friends and decades later in the Palliative Care Prayer Shawl Project, Montefiore Medical Center, Bronx, New York. While working as a Palliative Care Chaplain, I wanted to provide another form of comfort, along with additional support to patients that were anxious, and devastated by their illness, and who were far from home or had no family.

44

Doing further research on the subject, I came across "Prayer Shawl Ministry," a project started in 1998 by Janet Severi Bristow and Victoria Cole Galo, two graduates of the 1997 Women's Leadership Institute at The Hartford Seminary in Hartford, Connecticut. It has become an internationally known project. The spiritual practice of prayer is incorporated into the knitting or crocheting of the shawl, which embraces the recipient and or patient with comfort, love and solace. It has a dual benefit, because the process of making the shawl centers the crafter and the person receiving it!

Compassion and the love of knitting and/or crocheting have been combined into a prayerful ministry and spiritual practice, which reaches out to those in need of comfort and solace, as well as in celebration and joy. Many blessings are prayed into every stitch.

So how does one initiate a prayer shawl project within the largest urban medical center in the Bronx, New York? I presented the idea to Dr. Peter Selwyn, Chairperson of the Family and Social Medicine (DFSM) and overseer of the Palliative Care Service, and he accepted the project. I started making the prayer shawls in my office, due to restrictions of the hospital.

One day, while I attended a workshop, there was a woman sitting across from me crocheting. I approached her during our break and told her about the prayer shawl project (she was a Critical Care RN in one of our hospitals) and she got very excited to participate and even recruited some of the nurses she knew to also get involved.

An annual Blessing Ceremony was initiated in the chapel of the hospital in order for the chaplains and community faith leaders representing different faith to say a blessing/prayer over the prayer shawls that were made. Additionally, each prayer shawl was sprinkled with the Alpha & Omega anointing oil that I have been blending (the patients love the fragrance). We also give recognition to all the yarn donors and shawl makers, as well as the Palliative Care team members from our three campuses, who request the shawls for their patients.

Patient M – 1st recipient

- First seen in the Palliative care clinic in October 2013. She presented as a 52 y/o woman with stage IV R breast cancer she had been initially diagnosed in

12/2011 and had progressed through multiple lines of chemotherapy.

- She had just completed whole brain radiation therapy and had started on another round of targeted chemotherapy.
- Over the course of the next 12 months, through more chemotherapy and radiation, she maintained her wish to return home to her large family in the Caribbean Islands "when it was her time to die."
- She eventually developed spinal metastases and was admitted with a cord compression to Einstein hospital. She was transferred from there to Moses in order to complete radiation and at this time there were no more options for chemotherapy.

As the Prayer Shawl project developed, we had several nurses, colleagues from the hospital, community groups, and individuals who heard about the project and myself. I must highlight some like Marie Bonner who regularly shipped boxes of shawls and the Parkchester Knitting and Crochet Club who delightfully took us on as one of their main projects. In the four years of the Prayer Shawl Project more than three hundred prayer shawls were given to patients, family members and patients from our out-patient clinics. Through the years we have also received tremendous support from the Caregivers Support Centers in our Moses campus led by director Randi Kaplan, and Lynette Olmo program assistant, who even coordinated a wedding ceremony for one of our Palliative Care patients. I served as the marriage officiant and the bride wore her prayer shawl as her veil! At our Weiler campus led by Julie List and Lourdes Cruz, Sr. Secretary, we even conducted a Blessing Ceremony for the Prayer Shawls, in their center. Lourdes Cruz was the person who introduced the Parkchester Knitting and Crochet Club to the project and they generously supplied us with prayer shawls.

Hospice: A Historical Perspective

The term "hospice" (from the same linguistic root as "hospitality") can be traced back to medieval times when it referred to a place of shelter and rest for weary or ill travelers on a long journey. The name was first applied to specialized care for dying patients by physician Dame Cicely Saunders, who began her work with the terminally ill in 1948 and eventually went on to create the first modern hospice—St. Christopher's Hospice—in a residential suburb of London.

When we experience doubtfulness, trauma and pain all that is needed is the ministry of presence – no words are needed. Working in the HIV/AIDS epidemic and as chaplain in palliative care the ministry of presence was a priority and will continue to be in my journey of sowing hope!

Chapter 4

Memories of Healing and Loss

---

*"Whom have I in heaven but you?
And there is nothing on earth that I
desire besides you. My flesh and
my heart may fail, but God is the
strength of my heart and my
portion forever…But for me it is
good to be near God; I have made
the Lord God my refuge and my
portion forever."*
Psalm 73:25,26,28 (ESV)

A few years ago, during one of the teaching sessions at the Palliative Care Service, one of the Palliative Care Fellows used the Portuguese word "*saudade.*" He said it is a mixture of longing for a person, place or pretty much anything in the world and nostalgia for someone or something that is no longer near or with you, whether absence is temporary or permanent. We often look back, letting memories fill our minds, and hearts, then tears of joy and sorrow emerge. I am sharing with you my encounters with healing and loss.

I was too young to remember Cayey, Puerto Rico where our family lived. Both my parents were born there. Soon, in 1956, my father was stationed in Little Rock, Arkansas. I missed our family in Puerto Rico greatly. A few years later we had to leave Little Rock, Arkansas to go to Fayetteville, North Carolina and I missed the porch swing and my first American friend, Stephanie, in Little Rock. Then came the big move to the Bronx, New York in 1959. And, I missed the lakes, grass, trees and walking barefoot everywhere in Fort Bragg, North Carolina.

Sometime in the late 1960's, I started to count my losses after a family vacation drive from New York to North Carolina. I had left my parakeet with my cousins to care for it. When we returned home to New York, my cousin tearfully informed me that my bird had died. I knew it wasn't their fault, because they took very good care of their dog, Skippy, but for me it seemed that the possession I brought from North Carolina was lost!

While in New York, my father was sent to Germany and we couldn't go with him, because it was his last overseas station. I was afraid that I would lose my father with him being so far away. My sister Rachel's lung collapsed and was hospitalized, and then I got the measles. Rachel's teacher advocated to the American Red Cross on our behalf, so that my father could return home. Security! Again, our family moved, from the Hunts Point section in the Bronx, where I had a great group of cross-cultural friends from Cuba, Ireland, Israel, West Indies and Spain to the South Bronx section of the Bronx to housing projects with 21 floors. Thank God we lived on the fourth floor!

My maternal grandmother Amelia Torres Rodriguez, ("abuelita"), was the first bi-coastal person I knew. She spent winters in Cayey, Puerto Rico and all the other seasons in New York with us. My grandmother and I shared a bedroom and were extremely close. I loved her so much. She would tell me stories about working in the coffee and sugar cane fields, and how her family survived the great hurricane in Puerto Rico. Then, because of all the years of chewing tobacco, she developed cancer.

It was difficult seeing how cancer ravaged her body when she was sent to Calvary Hospital. She no longer was the jovial, little woman who comforted and spoiled me. Losing my *abuelita* was one of my first great losses in life. I missed the smell of her Maja perfume, mixed with the chewing tobacco she hid in her beautiful cotton handkerchief. Interestingly, I started carrying a colorful cotton handkerchief with me, except that mine carries the scent of anointing oil. But, that's another story I will tell you about later!

August of 2005, my sister Rachel and her husband, Joe, had a time share in Ft. Lauderdale, Florida and they wanted me and my middle sister, Amy, and her husband, Jesus, to join them, because we had been grieving Hermes' death. It was a beautiful resort, with great food and sightseeing. One morning, we headed out for a beach day. I decided to go on the water with the boogie board, and soon the waves started to swell. As I started to paddle back to shore, I felt my 25th wedding anniversary band slip off my finger into the ocean water! Panic set in! Grief overwhelmed me again! Everyone in the area tried to help; I couldn't see underwater because my eyes were filled with tears. A young boy told me, I will try to find it for you as he had a snorkel mask, but to no avail. Another loss in Florida!

Now you may say, "It's just a ring, no great loss, a ring can be replaced."

Yeah, yeah, blah, blah, what is it with me and losses? Why must I be given things and then have them taken away by loss? People, places, and even body parts! Menopause and grief is what I am experiencing now, and they aren't great company on what was supposed to be a healing get away. Talk about complicated grief!

So, I return to my room, sat on the porch and began to journal all my losses. My parents had come to live with us in 1982, because caregiving for my mother had become difficult for my father, alone in Puerto Rico. My mother had diabetes, cardiac issues, and renal failure. She was on dialysis, so my father had to take her three times a week, drive two hours to the dialysis clinic, wait for four hours of treatment and then drive another two hours back to their home in Carolina, Puerto Rico.

Thanksgiving eve November 1984, my father and I were busy prepping our Thanksgiving feast. I call it that because besides our immediate family, we included people from our church that had no family to join us. My mother had other plans that day and tried convincing my father and I to take her to a department store, because she wanted to buy a pair of "black shoes." We told her we couldn't, so she got on the phone and called my husband at the church and asked him to take her. He said yes, but by the time he got home the store was closed. Before mom went to bed, she told us to make sure we saved the turkey neck for her to have when she returned from dialysis treatment. On Thanksgiving morning, my father awakened me to check on my mother, because she wasn't responding. As I rushed to her room, she was laying in the bed peacefully, as if she was still sleeping, except there was no pulse and she wasn't breathing. She had drawn her last breath and left us just the way she said she wanted to die, at home, in her sleep, with family! The paramedics were amazed that a woman with her medical issues expired so peacefully. I believe it was God's grace, because she had suffered so much. We returned to her birthplace, Cayey, Puerto Rico, to lay her to rest in the family burial plot. Returning to Puerto Rico would be forever different.

Then it was my father who became bi-coastal, traveling from New York to Atlanta, Georgia with my sister, Amy, and her family, and then to Cayey, Puerto Rico. He went back and forth, until he remarried in 1990 and then remained in Puerto Rico.

The 1990's brought a series of yearly losses. One Sunday in June 1991, me and my daughters, Ruth and Tirzah, went out for lunch with some friends from church. I hesitated, because I would miss my usual Sunday afternoon phone call from my father. That evening, when I tried to call his home, no one answered the phone. Monday morning, I went to work, and strangely the receptionist called to say that someone was there to see me. My husband, Hermes, and church member, Scotty, appeared at my office to tell me that my father had just died in Puerto Rico. Another mournful trip to Cayey, Puerto Rico, same church, same funeral home, same cemetery. Please don't play Taps (my father was a

Korean and WWII veteran), and no gun salute. His army buddies folded his flag and presented it to his wife. His nephew, our dear cousin, Rev. Angel Luis Gutierrez, did the committals and encouraged us to leave, before they lowered the casket. Leaving my father there left me with a huge hole in my soul – being the youngest child, we had a very special relationship. I was the only child that has a middle name, Julia, because his name is Julio!

Again, Puerto Rico would never be the same. The people who brought me in this world were now buried in our homeland. I became an orphan in my homeland, "*mi tierra.*" I was glad I was born in San Juan, Puerto Rico, because I could go to "Old San Juan" with no sad memories.

My husband's youngest brother, Joel (Jay-Jay), had been incarcerated for drug possession and he also had AIDS. We had been advocating for a compassionate release, and in November 1993 he was released. Jay-Jay stayed with us, but soon after, he had to be admitted to the hospital, because he'd developed Pneumococcal pneumonia. His weakened immune system didn't allow him to recuperate and, sadly, on December 1, 1993, he died on World AIDS Day. We were very close, and my daughters adored him, so we were all grieving. They say in every dark moment we can also see hope arise, and for us it came when the Chief of Staff from the Bronx Borough President's Office came to the funeral home to pay his respects and in turn offered my husband a job as Director of Community Affairs.

In 1994, we had to leave our residence at the church parsonage – a beautiful Victorian, three-story home – and move into an apartment a few blocks away. One more loss on the list.

My husband's second youngest brother, David, had been combatting complications from AIDS and aggressive cancer. He died July 1994. Again, our family mourned the loss of a dear brother, talented musician, father to three daughters and husband to Sonia.

Then, in 1995, I had to be hospitalized with acute gallbladder disease and developed many complications during surgery. One evening, my father-in-law, Hermes Sr., was my last visitor in the hospital. We had a great relationship, and always played jokes on each other. Before he left, he patted my foot and told me to make sure I stayed in bed and winked! He went home and told his wife he didn't feel well. My husband checked on him, and they called 911. Sadly, he was pronounced dead in the emergency room, a few levels below where I was in the hospital. My husband came to my room the next morning with my sister, Rachel, and my doctor to tell me "Pa" went to be with the Lord. I was hysterically crying in my husband's arms! Since I was still hospitalized, I couldn't attend his funeral or burial. My grief was overwhelming me and the rest of our family.

I can't even tell you the number of funerals, memorial services and burials my husband and I conducted for persons that died from HIV/AIDS. We read their names every year on World AIDS Day, during Bruised Reed Ministry's Candlelight and Healing Service.

As I shared in an earlier chapter, in 2005 I lost my husband, Hermes. While living and working in the Bronx, NY, I would often come across people that had either attended one of the churches he pastored, was a colleague in ministry or worked with him. They would always share their memories of him. Mel

Lawrenz writes in his book, *A Chronicle of Grief*, *"Traumatic grief will take a person on a journey that is intense and painful and unpredictable. That is all normal. Supportive friends and family need to be a compassionate presence and not try to fix things. Grief is not a problem to be fixed but a process to be lived out."*

January 2009, while finishing my last semester at Alliance Theological Seminary, I enrolled in a two-week intensive course in Israel, led by one of my professors, Dr. Steven Notley. While we were in Jerusalem, at the Mount of Olives, we went to a church, Dominus Flevit, a Byzantine monastery, also known as *The Sanctuary of Jesus Weeping over Jerusalem*. One of the towers was in the shape of a tear. Being there, it reminded me of one of my husband Hermes' classic sermons entitled, "Tears are the Language God Understands," based on Luke 19:41-44 and Psalm 56:8 (NLT), *"You have kept track of all my sorrows. You have collected my tears in your bottle. You have recorded each one in your book."* The priest read these same passages and I became very emotional, my eyes welled up with tears and I walked out of the church. Some of the students got concerned and told our

Dean, Dr. Luis Carlo, who told them I would be okay. Dr. Carlo was familiar with the sermon of my late husband, because they were colleagues in ministry and family friends. The garden outside had a well that was filled by a pitcher that overflowed into it by the rain. It was a great comforting experience, that I was able to share with my classmates.

Then, there was the loss of our beloved Pookie.

Our dog Pookie, a Shih-Tzu/Chihuahua mixed breed, was given to my daughter, Tirzah, in 2001, when he was 6 months old. I was concerned, because we all suffered from allergies. We were allergic to cats and some dogs. Mimi the nurse practitioner that I worked with told me to give the dog a month, since his breed mix didn't have long fur or shed. Pookie slept with Ruth and Tirzah in their room, and he became part of the family.

As Pookie grew, he decided Hermes was his favorite. We spoiled him. My brother-in-law, Joe, made him this awesome step-up bench, so Pookie could go up to the living room windowsill and look out the window to the street. It quickly became his nap spot. He would get excited when he saw a white SUV, because he thought it was my sister, Rachel, picking us up to go to her house. He loved running in their backyard. After Hermes died in 2005, Pookie became very sad and decided he wanted to sleep with me, and we comforted each other. When my daughters moved out on their own, it was just us.

Pookie started getting sluggish and then had some seizures. I took him to the veterinarian, who said they would keep him overnight for observation and would update me on his condition. The next morning, I was at a funeral service for Gilbert, my dear friend Miriam Mathews' husband. I was to conduct the burial service later that day. While I was at the funeral home, the veterinarian's office called me to please come immediately, because Pookie was critical. When I got there, the veterinarian and his technician told me that it would be best to let him go and they felt I would understand, because I worked in palliative care. They let me have the room alone with him. I recorded a video of him, while he was still alert, for my daughters. The technician, who always took care of Pookie, told me she would stay with him as they put him down. I lost my dear companion a few months before his 15th birthday. He was cremated. My family, friends and neighbors all shared the loss and gave me support. Pookie died June 10, 2016.

A few days later, I received a call regarding Shanin. She grew up at Glad Tidings Church and was the one teenager we entrusted to babysit our daughters. She also did her AmeriCorps internship at BRM with me for a couple of years. She was the one that gave me the hearts that I put on the hope sign. Shanita, as we called her, was battling end-stage cancer in a hospice unit in NYC. When I went to see her, she told me, "You know what is happening" and we cried as I anointed her and prayed. On June 17, 2016, Shanita went to be with the Lord.

Through the years, I have experienced God's mercy, which has allowed me to walk alongside people in their journey of suffering, death, grief, healing and restoration. Psalm 147:3 (NLT) says, *"He heals the broken-hearted and bandages their wounds."*

Chapter 5

Sowing Hope

"Comfort and strength come from three powerful spiritual drugs: Faith, Hope and Love. My experience is that when combined with each other, they work synergistically and produce greater results. I hope, by now, you have had some moving experience that renewed your belief in Faith, Hope and Love. Experiencing these three spiritual realities can produce a deep feeling of wellbeing and purpose in life, feelings of comfort and strength." William Josef Dobbels. S.J.; An Epistle of Comfort, Scriptural Meditations and Passages for Person Suffering from AIDS

The term "Sowing Hope" came to me in prayer after reading Romans 15:13 (ESV), "May the God of hope fill you with all joy and peace in believing, so that by the power of the Holy Spirit you may abound in hope." As I lead Bruised Reed Ministry, this verse became integral to fulfilling the mission to persons afflicted, affected or abandoned, because of HIV/AIDS. During our years of pastoring Glad Tidings Church, we had many young people that were graffiti artists, and one of them told me "Sowing Hope" should be my tag line (the term they used for signing their graffiti). So, it became my signage until this day!

Now, I want to share with you a portion of my seminary study entitled: "Hope and Suffering," so you can get a better understanding of my journey of "Sowing hope."

"Hope and Suffering." I see them as synergistic partners; they work together – not against each other. Romans 5:3-5(ESV), "...but we also rejoice in our sufferings, because we know that suffering produces perseverance; perseverance, character, and character, hope. And hope does not disappoint us, because God has poured out his love into

66

our hearts by the Holy Spirit, whom he has given us." Suffering and hope enhance our lives. They provide inner healing. This inner healing radically changes the quality of your life for the better and forever.

My experience and research on suffering and hope began in the early 1980's when my mother was diagnosed with renal failure, co-factors of diabetes and heart disease. The strain of the two-hour drive each way to take my mother three times a week, wait there until the four hours of dialysis treatment finished, was slowly affecting my father as well. It was then that we had to relocate my parents, after their retirement to our homeland Puerto Rico, so they could move in with me at our home in the Bronx.

My mother's outlook in this illness was amazing and she attributed it to the hope of one day living without any disease in the Presence of the Lord. She utilized every moment of her dialysis treatment to witness and conduct mini Bible study sessions with the persons sitting next to her and the technicians who took care of her! One day, while sitting in the renal specialists' office waiting for my mother, I read an article in the NY Times about border babies

– babies suffering with AIDS that were abandoned by their families. I wanted to adopt one of these children even though I was about to give birth to my youngest child. My husband said, "No way, you already have your hands full with our daughters, your parents, and the boys (we were raising from the church) as well." As I shared earlier, on Thanksgiving morning of 1984 the Lord gave my mother the desire on her heart and took her to be with Him, while she slept!

The next year, during a preaching series based on Isaiah 42:3, our church started Bruised Reed Ministry, a para-church ministry for those afflicted and affected by HIV/AIDS. I too received the desire of my heart to sow hope – into the lives of those suffering from AIDS. This work, and move of the Spirit, received inspiration from Romans 15:13.

Suffering

We all experience suffering in our lives. The cause of pain and suffering can be emotional, psychological, physiological, and even spiritual, whether it is due from abuse (physical/mental), disease, stress or disobedience to God's word. At creation, we were given life; childbirth became painful because of the fall, a form of suffering. In Christ, we experience redemption that will bring us, according to Revelation 21:1-4; 22:1-5, eternal healing and wholeness. Most people have seen human suffering as inevitable – a 'fact of life' – but not as a theological issue, still less as a possible barrier to faith in a beneficent God.

The suffering of Job in the Old Testament resurfaces continuously as an example of extreme suffering, the physical pain of illness and the emotional pain of loss of family. In the same account, we also find out that most of our "friends" don't know how to comfort us when we are suffering or in pain. Job's hope is in Yahweh and this is what makes him a survivor.

During the time I served as chaplain for the HIV Palliative Care Team at Montefiore Medical Center, I had the opportunity to attend several conferences and trainings in end-of-life care. At one of the trainings, I met Daniel P Sulmasy, O.F.M., M.D., a priest who became a physician and often lectures on spirituality and health. In his book, *The Healer's Calling*, he dedicates a chapter on suffering and says the following: "Suffering, on the other hand, is something very different from pain. Suffering is experienced in relation to one's situation in life. So, to understand what it means to suffer, one must understand what it means to be human. No wonder then, that suffering has been called a mystery. It is as deep as the mystery of being human."

My observance in working in palliative care is that all of humanity, all ethnic groups and all cultures are affected by suffering. All have different coping mechanisms to deal with either pain or suffering. The patients who had no form of belief system struggled with severe pain and voiced their suffering with anger towards God who would, "Put them through this!" Those who had some faith in God would express that they prayed God would see them through this experience. The knowledge of the fact that hope would see them through would give them peace in their lives, no matter how much more time they had to live.

F.P. Cotterell, who writes the section on Suffering in the New Dictionary of Biblical Theology, divides the subject by Old and New

Testaments. The following is my brief highlights of his points:

Ecclesiastes: Tears of the oppressed.

Isaiah: Unidentified sufferer for all people.

Job: "Treatise of suffering."

Synoptic Gospels: Sufferings of Christ.

John: Jesus' encounter with the blind man.

Romans: Universality of suffering by creation.

Corinthians: Pain of illness, accident or violence.

Timothy: Persecution as a consequence of Christianity.

Hebrews: It is inescapable.

In Harold Koenig's book, *The Healing Power of Faith* (Simon & Shuster), he shares that the medical and scientific communities are studying how people cope when they are suffering with pain and illness. They have become intrigued with the power of faith, hope and prayer in relation to a patient's diagnosis, illness, and recovery. Over the years, Duke University's Center for the Study of Religion/Spirituality and Health's scientists have led more than 50 major research projects on the relationship between faith and health. More than 70 data-based, peer-reviewed papers published in medical and scientific journals have resulted from these projects. Many of the center's studies have produced groundbreaking findings:

- People who regularly attend church, pray individually, and read the Bible have significantly lower diastolic blood pressure than the less religious. Those with the lowest blood pressure both attend church and pray or study the Bible often.
- People who attend church regularly are hospitalized much less often than people who never or rarely participate in religious services.
- People with strong religious faith are less likely to suffer depression from stressful life events, and if they do, they're more likely to recover from depression than those who are less religious.

In my research on the subject of suffering, I came across this excellent outline and wanted to include it in totality. Elisabeth Elliot, in her book, *A Path through Suffering* (Michigan, Servant Publications), provides an appendix entitled: "A Summary of Reasons for Suffering" and divides the experience into four categories:

- **We suffer for our own sake:** That we may learn to trust: 2 Corinthians 1:8-9; To produce in us endurance, character, hope: Romans 5:3-4
- **We suffer for the sake of God's people**: That grace may extend more: 2 Corinthians 4:15; That our generosity may bless others: 2 Corinthians 8:2
- **We suffer for the world's sake:** That the life of Jesus may be visible in ordinary human flesh: 2 Corinthians 4:10
- **We suffer for Christ's sake:** That we may identify with Him in His crucifixion: Galatians 2:20; of faith: Psalms 44:22; Acts 9:16 and 14:22; 2 Timothy 3:12; John 15:18-21; 1 Thessalonians 1:6 and 3:4.

One summer, at Crossroads Tabernacle Church in Bronx, New York (the church I attended) I had the opportunity to hear Max Lucado read his newest book aloud, *John 3:16 The Numbers of Hope*, in our church. Lucado calls this scripture "A twenty-six-word parade of hope: beginning with God, ending with life, and urging us to do the same." Psalm 23:4 and John 3:16 summarize the fact that we will all come in contact with hope and suffering in our life's journey. However, the key lies in believing that God walks with us in the valley, so we 'will not fear.' It is in knowing God's love and salvation through Christ that provides our assurance of 'everlasting life,' which changes the outcome of our suffering and strengthens our hope. Max Lucado, *John 3:16 The Numbers of Hope*, (Tennessee, Thomas Nelson, 2007)

"There is such an enormous hunger for meaning in life, for comfort and consolation, for forgiveness and reconciliation, for restoration and healing, that anyone who has any authority in the Church should constantly be reminded that the best word to characterize religious authority is compassion. Let's keep looking at Jesus, whose authority was expressed in compassion." Henri Nouwen

Jesus has compassion for all who are suffering as we see in Matthew 9: 35-36. The Latin root for the word 'compassion' is *pati*, which means "to suffer," and the prefix *com* means "with," so compassion literally means "with-suffering."

Our compassion must be to those who are afflicted, affected and abandoned. It is to these that we must make a covenant to "Sow Hope!" Two specific passages of scripture have encouraged me in my own journey of "Sowing Hope" and they are Jeremiah 29:11, given to me by the publisher of my book when my husband died, and Acts 2:26, in the Message Bible, that says, "I have pitched my tent in the land of hope."

HOPE

Hope is an essential tool, which allows us to cope and thrive through various experiences in life. The New Dictionary of Biblical Theology (Illinois: Intervarsity Press, 2000) says; "In difficult circumstances, hope provides a bubble-like safe place in which to exist for the time being." Often, if not always, it is a personal experience, because when it is shared with others, as in the case of Job in the Old

Testament or the woman with the issue of blood in the New Testament, we are considered as strange, or not fully there. Having hope is a very conscious state of mind and scriptures, such as 1 Corinthians 13:13, associate hope with faith and love. Sadly, many people live with hopelessness, because they don't know Jesus Christ, who provides us with this hope, according to Romans 5:2-5.

Hope – "A biblical term (Greek elpis) referring to the expectation of the belief that God will fulfill promises made in the past. Biblical hope is more than a simple wish; it entails certainty based on God's demonstration of faithfulness to people in the history of salvation as recorded in the Scriptures and as experienced by the church. Ultimately, the Christian's future hope lies in the promise of Christ's return and the anticipation of resurrection from the dead."

H – HEALING

O – OVERCOMING

P – PERSEVERING

E – ENDURANCE

The preceding is an acronym written for the spiritual formations group I lead, "Sowing Hope," at Crossroads Tabernacle in Bronx, New York. As I shared earlier, my ministry service and research has not only been in HIV/AIDS but in the connection that health and spirituality have in our world. In the book, *A Hard Fought Hope*, the authors Long and Carney, state: "Significant figures in the Western philosophical and religious world have made hope an important category of their thought. Immanuel Kant...stated that the weightiest questions for him to answer in all of his works... "For what may I hope?" Thomas Aquinas, the 13th-century Christian theologian, defined hope as, "A specialized desire characterized by a specialized object. The object of hope must be clearly good, apparent in the future, difficult or arduous to attain but regarded as possible to attain."

In Larry Vandecreek's book, *Spiritual Needs and Pastoral Services, Readings in Research*, (Oregon, Journal of Pastoral Care Publications, 1995), he states that many researchers view hope as a psychological variable that can enhance relationships with others and with God or a "higher power"; serve as a coping mechanism and increase our belief system. In fact, Dr. Craig Ellison of Alliance Graduate School of Counseling developed a Spiritual Well-Being Scale (SWB) that is utilized with patients in many therapeutic settings and hospitals. "Ellison (1983) views hope as an integral part of the SWB that would help enable a person to find purpose and meaning beyond the immediate situation and to relate positively to God."

Hope helps a person develop resilience, along with the ability to be flexible and bounce back from the circumstance he or she is facing. Hope gives us purpose, as well as the courage and strength to overcome fear. We become proactive when we have hope, by not letting the crisis we are in devastate or hinder us from surviving. Hope gives us the assurance that all things come to pass, and we continue onward because of Christ. The authors of the New Dictionary of Biblical Theology state, "Hope is an ultimate reality, giving shape and meaning to the present, is a distinguishing feature of Christians; unbelievers 'have no hope' according to 1 Thessalonians 4:13; Ephesians 2:12. Paul, looked forward to being 'with Christ'; Christ's presence was Paul's hope. Hope is like a safety net, the presence of which encourages us to take risks. *Deus Spei* ('the

God of Hope'). What makes the content of biblical hope distinctive is that God meets us (more than) halfway."

Having experienced many instances of pain and loss has strengthened me to develop resilience. Knowing that God had chosen me, and He loves me unconditionally is another spiritual motivator, because it has developed a grateful attitude, an attitude of faith and expectancy. Inner healing radically changes the quality of your life for the better and forever. Hope, love and faith work synergistically. They are the antidote for a sick soul, an afflicted body, a tormented mind, and a cynical spirit.

Alpha & Omega Anointing Oil

Many years ago, while experiencing a life tragedy a dear friend brought someone to pray for me, she anointed me and gave me a beautiful perfume bottle filled with the anointing oil. Since that day I continue the process which requires blending, crushing the cassia, frankincense, myrrh and olive oil. Adding centered prayer for the healing virtue to flow from heaven to the person whose faith can bring wholeness.

My husband Hermès used to refer our daughters Ruth and Tirzah as Alpha and Omega. Years later a friend suggested that should be the name "Alpha &Omega"

Now that I am a widow, the account of the prophet Elijah telling the widow that her supply will always be there because she served him, has become mine as well. This oil has traveled to many places as a balm of Gilead and continues my mission of Sowing Hope.

Many vacillate between hope and despair. Faith strengthens our resolve. Resolve is the key to victory and helps us endure our circumstance. Hope flourishes and gives us the fortitude to bear our pain and suffering. Psalm 119:116117 says, "Uphold me according to your promise, that I may live, and let me not be put to shame in my hope! Hold me up, that I may be safe and have regard for your statutes continually!"

Hope has been what has kept me in all the issues of life I have experienced, including pain, suffering, grief, and loneliness. This year, 2020, we are experiencing the worldwide pandemic of the coronavirus, COVID-19, an indiscriminate epidemic. We have become familiar with continually-used terms such as: quarantine, isolation, shelter in place, social distancing, wash your hands for 20 seconds, and wear your mask. Cities have been shut down. As I am writing this book, worldwide cases of COVID-19 reached 34 million and sadly 1.01 million deaths. Churches have had to close and depend on technology to minister. Family members were separated, our sick loved ones couldn't be held, burials/funerals couldn't be conducted.

This past March, I was scheduled on a flight to New York to celebrate my oldest daughter Ruth's 40th birthday and attend a clergy conference of the Council of Holistic Christian Churches and Ministry, with whom I belong to, for my ministerial credentialing. It saddened me to cancel this trip, because of COVID-19. The cases in New York were extremely high, so my daughter didn't want me to put myself at risk (because of my age and respiratory issues). My heart ached for how the borough of the Bronx, where I had lived for more than 50-plus years and the hospital where I had once worked, and where my youngest daughter works, was overwhelmed with cases and deaths due to COVID-19. Prayers of intercession were non-stop. Psalm

91 being prayed over my oldest daughter, Ruth (working in a charter school), her children Kaleb and Phoenix, who attended school in the Bronx, and my youngest daughter, Tirzah (working at Montefiore Hospital), and all my family and friends back in New York, as well as my current community.

May 15, 2020, I watched a CBS special called *Bravery and Hope: 7 Days on the Frontline*. News journalists followed the emergency physicians, critical care specialists, and nurses at Montefiore Medical Center in the Bronx during the height of the pandemic. I worked at this very hospital, located a few blocks from where I once lived and for more than 10 years served as a Palliative Care Chaplain. My eyes filled with tears as I saw the perseverance of the EMT, nurses, ER staff, Critical Care, and Palliative Care teams treat their patients. I wanted to be present with them, to offer prayers of hope and encouragement. But, instead, I did so via prayer in my home, along with text messages and phone calls! Our souls shrivel when we are tired and weary. We all struggle with balance and the stress that struggle creates.

One of my former Palliative Care team social workers, Ken Meeker, LMSW, and I did a teaching: *Burnout: The Road to Disenchantment* and *Self-Care: The Key to Longevity*. He has given me permission to share some of the teaching points.

Burnout is the gradual process by which a person, in response to prolonged stress and physical, mental, and emotional strain, detaches from work and other meaningful relationships. The result is lowered productivity, cynicism, confusion…a feeling of being drained and having nothing more to give.

In order to manage stress, we must:

- Slow down; take pauses.
- Decide what's important to you and what's not?
- Be mindful of what you can control and what you can't – stop worrying!
- Acknowledge the gifts we're given.
- Change your routine.
- Cognitive Behavioral Therapy (CBT) – Use self-talk to counter negative cognitions; a mistake does not mean failure; recall success.

I added that regularly refreshing ourselves is not a sign of weakness or selfishness – it's the way to stay healthy emotionally, physically, and spiritually. Focus is always found when you take time to stop, take inventory of the demands upon your time, and begin investing the best part of your day praying, meditating, loving your loved ones, and looking at the beauty of nature. These practices have been essential to our well-being and this current pandemic has given many of us the opportunity to do so while we are sheltering or quarantined at home. Ann Voskamp writes in her book, *The Broken Way*, "Not one thing in your life is more important than figuring out how to live in the face of unspoken pain."

Healers are in need of healing as we continue to be faced with the current pandemic and other illnesses. "Sow Hope!"

Chapter 6

Caring for Souls

"We keep healing as we keep being healers. In being the gift of healing for someone's brokenness, we receive a gift of healing for our own brokenness… Co-suffering with the suffering is how Jesus chose to literally transform the suffering." Ann Voskamp, Be The Gift.

Sometime ago I started collecting hearts. People started giving them to me, because they knew I loved them. A summer intern, volunteering at our church, gave me her heart ring "Just because," she said, "you gave me love." The collection included heart-shaped tea candles, earrings, mugs, sunglasses, letter openers, crosses with hearts, t-shirts, and it goes on and on. I have been broken-hearted, but my heart continues to beat. People share their heartache with me, because as they tell me, "I feel you will understand." Psalm 147:3 (NIV), "He heals the broken-hearted and bandages their wounds."

The large picture window in our living room faced the Museum of Bronx History. On that windowsill, I had a gold wooden HOPE sign. Laying on top of it were four red hearts, representing my daughters, Ruth and Tirzah, and my grandchildren, Kaleb and Phoenix. Since we lived on the second floor and in clear view of the main street that directly led from the "D" subway station to Montefiore Medical Center, it was my intention that people walking by could see it, search their hearts and have hope! C.H. Spurgeon said, "Hope itself is like a star not to be seen in the sunshine of prosperity and only to be discovered in the night of adversity."

"*Cura animarum*" in Latin means cure and care. Care for the whole person, body, mind and spirit. Soul Care deals with the pyscho-spiritual. The soul is where spirituality and psychology meet. This is also the place where the deepest levels of inner healing occur. The soul is the place where we get revitalized.

The Hebrew word "yasha" means to help, deliver, to remove or seek to remove someone from a burden of oppression or danger. "Chayah" means to preserve life, bring life, cause to live. This is soul care as seen in the following portion of scripture from Isaiah 58:5-12 (ESV), *"Is such the fast that I choose, a day for a person to humble himself? Is it to bow down his head like a reed, and to spread sackcloth and ashes under him? Will you call this a fast, and a day acceptable to the Lord?*

"Is not this the fast that I choose: to lose the bonds of wickedness, to undo the straps of the yoke, to let the oppressed go free, and to break every yoke?

Is it not to share your bread with the hungry and bring the homeless poor into your house; when you see the naked, to cover him, and not to hide yourself from your own flesh?

Then shall your light break forth like the dawn, and your healing shall spring up speedily; your righteousness shall go before you; the glory of the Lord shall be your rear guard.

Then you shall call, and the Lord will answer; you shall cry, and he will say, 'Here I am.' If you take away the yoke from your midst, the pointing of the finger, and speaking wickedness, if you pour yourself out for the hungry and satisfy the desire of the afflicted, then shall your light rise in the darkness and your gloom be as the noonday.

And the Lord will guide you continually and satisfy your desire in scorched places and make your bones strong; and you shall be like a watered garden, like a spring of water, whose waters do not fail.

And your ancient ruins shall be rebuilt; you shall raise up the foundations of many generations; you shall be called the repairer of the breach, the restorer of streets to dwell in."

Soul care involves making a covenant with God and the individual to nurture, support, comfort, and commit to restoration. Wounded souls are walking by us, we see them, hear them speak but never hear them cry themselves to sleep. Plagued by betrayal, rejection, ostracized by their family, friends and their church. Anger, bitterness and shame wells up in their souls. I have listened to so many people tell me they no longer go to church or believe in God, because of the negative church experiences or the neglect/abandonment they felt from faith leaders they once heard preach.

Rejection has a way of sinking the spirit, it makes us angry, bitter, and leads us to isolation and we find it difficult to forgive or seek restoration with the people who have hurt us so deeply. I will be vulnerable with you and must confess, I have experienced this when my husband confessed, during a counseling session, that he had committed adultery with someone from the church. My world crashed! The Assemblies of God denomination that Glad Tidings Church belonged to forbade us from returning to the church for him to ask for forgiveness and seek restoration for our family. Our family was devastated, as we had served the Lord, the church and our community for 11 years.

My children's lives were deeply affected, because all their friends were from the church. Our youngest daughter wasn't permitted to continue her education at the Christian Academy and we had to enroll her in our local public school. She cried every day as I walked her to the new school.

Bruised Reed Ministry, the HIV/AIDS ministry that was birthed at this church, was deeply affected, because we now were homeless, since I couldn't be at the church! Since we lived in the church parsonage, they gave us a few months to find another place to live.

The Assemblies of God required us to be evaluated and sent us to their psychologist in Ohio for three days of intensive therapy sessions. Our dear friends, Pastors Leon and Marylin Campbell (Marylin and I have been friends since we were five years old), let us stay with them while we were in Ohio, which was additionally instrumental for our marriage, because they provided support throughout the healing process. Hermes took a sabbatical from ministry for a year and we continued healing through therapy and prayer, and thanks to many family, friends, and colleagues in ministry that walked alongside us, providing love and support. My dear friend, Eva Pacheco, shared this with me: "The Lord uses the very negative things for good – healing and hope for others. When the Lord allows suffering in our lives, (as humans we all experience it in different ways), it's designed to help strengthen us and others. Like Jesus told

Peter, But I have prayed for you that your faith may not fail. And when you have turned again (are restored), strengthen your brothers Luke 22:32 (ESV). These experiences in our lives bring greater compassion and understanding for the suffering of others.

"I'm convinced that the most poignant and powerful moments in our lives, however, happen when God takes us through the instructional and developmental seasons of suffering. As a result, I am drawn to the lost and hurting. Yes, I'm an encourager and seek to inspire people, but my gift of exhortation sprouted in a dark place and was cut and trimmed by the Master's scalpel of life's difficulties." T.D. Jakes, *Crushing, God Turns Pressure into Power*.

One summer, in 2010, while attending the Leadership Summit, hosted by Crossroads Tabernacle in Bronx, New York, Reverend Mitchell Torres, from Harvest Field Community Church, told me that Glad Tidings Church had a new pastor. He was also attending the summit and had asked if he could arrange for us to have lunch together. The following day, we met up with Reverend Efraim Figueroa. He had recently been installed as pastor of Glad

Tidings Church and expressed that the Lord had put in his heart to have me come one Sunday in October during Pastor Appreciation Month. He felt that reconciliation was needed and asked if I would be willing to share a word of encouragement in the service and wanted my family to join me there. The church had several pastors come and go since we left in 1993.

The Lord used Pastor Efraim 17 years later to provide what the verse from Philippians 2:1 (NLT) states, "Is there any encouragement from belonging to Christ? Any comfort from his love? Any fellowship together in the Spirit? Are your hearts tender and compassionate?" Pastor Efraim's compassionate effort brought healing to us all, my daughters Ruth and Tirzah, my late husband's family, friends that had once attended Glad Tidings and wanted to support us that day and the body of Christ at the church. We were restored again!

Max Lucado, in his current book, *You Are Never Alone*, shares the following: "No one makes it through life failure-free. No one. Peter didn't. Jacob didn't. King David didn't. Solomon didn't. I haven't, and you won't. There is within each of us the capacity to do the very thing we resolve to avoid … Jesus still gives what he gave Peter: complete and total restoration."

The Lord has used many faith leaders to speak into my life when I experienced the relational tragedy of betrayal and to this day God is using others to encourage me. The following are my own personal life lessons in overcoming shame and unforgiveness and how healing and restoration got me to where I am today.

The Spirit of Encouragement: The purpose that enable one to withstand fear or difficulty.

---

2 Corinthians 1:3,4,7 (ESV),
"Blessed be the God and Father of
our Lord Jesus Christ, the Father
of mercies and God of all comfort,
who comforts us in all our
affliction, so that we may be able
to comfort those who are in any
affliction, with the comfort we
ourselves are comforted by God.
Our hope for you is unshaken, for
we know that as you share in your

*sufferings, you will also share in
our comfort."*

- Fear makes us weak, to bear the weak we must strengthen ourselves.
- Be a living demonstration of God's mercy.
- Courage gives us the ability to face past hurts.

The spirit of Endurance: The strength which allows one to carry on despite the difficulty.

---

*Psalm 119:49,50 (NIV),
"Remember the word to thy
servant in which you have made
me hope. This is my comfort in my
affliction. That your word has
revived me (preserved me alive)."*

- Affliction has awoken us; Holy Spirit is awakening us.

94

The Spirit of Empathy: The ability to identify and be involved with someone's situation, demonstrating sincerity and deep concern.

Galatians 6:2 (NIV), "Carry each other's burdens, ..."

- It is a form of grace, found in people who have experienced troubles.
- Focus on what they are telling you and what they are feeling.

The Spirit of Embracing: The compassion to love on one another.

Luke 6:31 (NASB), "Treat each other the same way you want them to treat you."

- Listen to God's voice of compassion.
- The weak and exhausted need to be encouraged, embraced and empowered to be able to endure this journey.

In 2001, I attended a seminar by Stanford University, "The Power of Forgiveness." One of the presenters was Everett L. Worthington Jr., Professor and Chair of Psychology, who was also Executive Director of the John Templeton Foundation's Campaign for Forgiveness. As researcher in forgiveness and reconciliation, he felt that restoration begins and ends with forgiveness of the actions of another or oneself. He outlined five steps for forgiveness and healing to occur, based on the acronym R. E. A. C. H. **Recall** the Hurt. **Empathize. Altruistic** gift of forgiveness. **Commit** to forgive. **Holding** onto forgiveness. After his teaching, many people remained in their seats. I believe they were trying to process their personal issues of forgiveness, or probably had just experienced restoration in their lives. We all need it and, as we receive restoration, others get freed from the strongholds in their own spirit as well. We can sing the spiritual: "Free at last, free at last, thank God Almighty, I'm free at last." I sang it that day and hope you can experience it as well.

That personal experience taught me courage and resilience. My personal challenge for you is to develop the spirit of encouragement, endurance, and empathy.

Then, embrace the opportunity to minister healing to those you may encounter in their journey of life. Guide them into restoration and peace with others and to God, who waits for them with open arms, so that they may find rest and refuge in our God Almighty.

Chapter 7

Transitions

"Take the first step in faith. You don't have to see the whole staircase, just take the first step."
Martin Luther King Jr.

We all face transitions in our lives. Websters Dictionary defines transition as a "passage from one state, stage, subject, or place to another; change."

"Life can only be understood backwards; but it must be lived forwards." - Soren Kierkegaard

During my childhood, it took place every time my father was stationed in another state during his service in the U.S. Army. Then, it was when I went from being a student, to seeking a career, marriage, motherhood, family and ministry, meshed with careers.

I have previously mentioned my dear "sister-friends" Eva and Marylin, both of whom became educators. We moved and eventually lived in different states. However, we remained connected by bus, car (not me I didn't start driving until the age of 65), train, plane, land line telephone, pen and paper. Now, after 60 years of friendship, we are all "retired" and all of us live in different states, so we communicate via email, text messages and cellphones! Our transitions have not affected the genuine love we have for each other, or the love for the God who brought us together and that we serve!

Widowhood was one of the biggest transitions in my life, as well as for many other men and women.

A few years ago, I read Afton Rorvik's book, Storm Sisters, Friends Through All Seasons. In her book, she states, "What if? We all struggle to recognize and admit our need. What might happen, if in just one friendship, you both found the courage to speak of your deep-down needs?"

I thought about some of the widows that I know and decided to purchase copies of Afton

Rorvik's book for each one of them, then have a dinner gathering in my apartment so that we would all have an opportunity to meet other women who are experiencing the transition of widowhood. We had a great time, eating and getting to know each other. Gathering in the living room, I gave them each a copy of the book *Storm Sisters, Friends Through All Seasons*. They agreed it should be our group name, because we all had experienced storms in our lives and were in transition.

They have given me permission to share who they are and how we met.

- Diane is a social worker. We met at Crossroads Tabernacle, but she shared we are really family! My husband's uncle was Diane's late husband's stepfather. Diane and her brothers founded Manna of Life, which I was involved with as well and we both worked for Montefiore Hospital.
- Soraya was married to my high school buddy Mario (we considered each other family). Mario and my husband worked

for the Bronx Borough President and we lived in the same neighborhood.

- Myrna attended Glad Tidings Church and knew my husband from the church in which he grew up. We both worked at Montefiore Hospital and lived in the same neighborhood.
- Miriam is a self-employed business-woman, a DJ, and was involved with Bruised Reed Ministry. She also served on the Covenant of Hope AIDS Taskforce and used to attend Crossroads Tabernacle before moving.
- Gladys worked in the hospitality industry, attended Crossroads Tabernacle and currently serves in several capacities with Manna of Life Ministries.
- Jane is a dental hygienist. We met when her husband was one of my Palliative Care patients. She later started attending Crossroads Tabernacle and we lived in the same neighborhood.

(In my capacity as Palliative Care chaplain, I had the privilege to walk alongside and care for the husbands and families of Gladys, Jane, Myrna and Soraya.)

Caregiving alters our lives as we once knew it. Challenges in life transform us.

Two of my Storm Sisters agreed to share their stories, so you can hear from other voices.

Gladys Roman: STORM SISTERS

Life without my husband, Tony is what I feared since I became his wife. Tony asked me to marry him three weeks after I met him. My friends and family begged me not to marry him so quickly. But, three months later we were married and expecting a baby. It was a bit scandalous, but we were so happy. Our marriage was good. My husband honored and respected me, and always took care of me. It took a while to really get to know each other but, once we were settled, life was good. Even though life was good, and we were super blessed, Tony and I loved to party, drink and hang out. Our kids were with us as we partied together and lived "*la vida loca*." God was so merciful. He kept us from harm and provided for us. As time went on though, we realized that things were not so good and we needed a change. A friend of ours, who partied heavily, invited us to church. We gave our hearts to Christ and began to understand how God's unfailing love and forgiveness was for us and available to all. The shame and guilt that we felt, the many years of immoral behavior, did not overtake us and our new life was great.

We were together 19 years, enjoying life, involved in church and serving our community when he started showing signs of memory loss and confusion. Two years later he was diagnosed with Alzheimer's disease. One year later, he noticed a lump under his arm and tested positive for cancer. Tony survived for another 12 years and passed away after the two diseases took over his body.

After my husband's death, I had to learn to live alone, without my partner, without my friend who always heard my cries. Many friends and family were very supportive and willing to help in anyway, yet I felt they did not really understand how much pain I was feeling and how sad I felt. I heard many words from folks who were not widows or widowers that were well intentioned, but actually caused more pain to my soul. I was overwhelmed with sadness and grief.

Reverend Rosa Caraballo invited a group of widows to have dinner in her home. Finally, I would be surrounded by a group of women who experienced the pain and suffering that I knew so well. Each story was so different, yet we were so connected, because of the death of our husbands. Some of us endured prolonged periods of caregiving, before losing our husbands and others had to deal with the sudden, unexpected death of their partners. After sharing my story, I felt like the ladies really understood and heard my pain. As I listened to their responses to my experience, I knew that they felt my pain. They never, ever said anything that I felt was insensitive and, finally, I felt heard. The dinners continued and the times we spent together are priceless memories that I will cherish forever. Thanks be to God for Sisters in Christ, especially Storm Sisters.

***

Jane Montalvo's Caregiving Experience.

Caregiving for someone with any type of dementia can be a heart-wrenching, exhausting experience. The responsibilities and tasks involved can often cause the caregiver to become filled with overwhelming emotions. This was the case for my family, when I became my husband's caregiver. My husband, Joe, was diagnosed with Early Onset Alzheimer's disease at age 46. At the time, our family of four included our two children, who were 10 and 12 years old. Throughout our journey, there were many sad and frightening moments but, there were also those rare sweet moments. When I reflect on some of those moments, I cry and smile, knowing that, through it all, my family was provided with divine strength and courage.

The hardest moments for me as the primary caregiver came with making decisions regarding my husbands' treatment plan, not being ready for the unexpected, and the feeling that I had made a mistake. One of those times was the morning Joe had his first seizure. It was a routine morning, getting Joe ready for adult day care and myself ready for work, when suddenly I heard a loud thump in our bedroom.

I ran, only to see him on the floor having a seizure. I panicked and called for my daughter whom took charge of the situation. She turned him, made sure he wasn't choking and somehow managed to dress him. After, initiating the 911 call, I explained to the medics that Joe was a retired member of the Emergency Medical Service with Alzheimer's. I handed them the list of his medications and, after getting him on the ambulance, I started shaking. The anxiety and fear I experienced at that moment was overwhelming. Later, in the emergency room, trying to explain to the medical staff that Joe had Alzheimer's and could not be left unattended for one moment was exhausting. The exhaustion came from having to repeat myself over and over. Doctors and staff would look at Joe in disbelief. My husband was a young, healthy man, so it's impossible for him to have Alzheimer's.

I wasn't ready at all for this phase of his illness. In anger, I questioned his doctors. Why wasn't I told this would happen? Why didn't they prepare me? Their response was that in Early Onset Alzheimer's, seizures are common, and it is unclear as to why they occur. I recall being more shocked than when we received his initial diagnosis. I questioned that, wasn't what my children and I going through enough? So, with the seizures, my sleepless nights would now become nights in which my children and I would be on continuous flight fright mode, as we lived in fear of him falling at any moment.

Over time, my children became parents to their dad, while helping provide guidance and care as best as they could. Along with this new role came more responsibilities. I worried for them day and night. I needed the physical, mental and spiritual endurance to keep going forward myself. I questioned whether I was doing the right thing for Joe's care, as well as the children.

As Joe continued to advance in this illness, he became fearful of taking walks in the park. So, one evening, I decided to take him for a walk around familiar territory. Having been an emergency medical technician (EMT) for Fire Department New York (FDNY), I knew that the hospital near our home would be familiar to him.

As we walked, along the perimeter of the hospital, I heard Joe say, "Thank you." Taking advantage of the lucid moment, I responded,

"For what, Joe?" He slowed his pace and looked at the pavement. And, pointing downward, he said, "For this, thank you." I knew, in that moment, that what Joe was trying to say was, "Jane, thank you for taking me on these walks, thank you for taking care of me." These words were enough to fill me with joy for a very long time. Those affirming words, which I desperately needed to hear, carried me through the remainder of our journey. Over time, Joe was unable to walk, dance, talk or see me. However, in the most difficult moments, in my heart, I kept hearing the words, "For this, thank you."

The morning Joe went to be with our Lord, I was with him. Oddly, it was a different nurse I had never seen before that bathed and groomed him. And, she was singing. She used her personal caddy of soaps, creams and powders. I believe she had been instructed to prepare Joe for his departure. When she was done, I sat him up as much as I could. The sunlight was shining in through the window and made his light brown eyes look like gold. He was frail and breathing slowly but Joe looked more handsome than I had seen him in a long time.

I wasn't in denial about what would be happening soon. I just didn't think it would happen that morning. When I noticed his breathing sounds change, I ran to get the doctor. He came in the room and announced that I had three minutes.

I took those moments to repeat the same words I said the night he was diagnosed. "Everything is going to be okay Joe. I promise to take care of Jonathan and Starr to the best of my ability. We will all be well."

For the first time in many months, He slightly turned his head and looked at me. In that moment, I got on my knees and cried. The doctor announced, one minute, and I cried harder. I managed to tell him that he was going to be in a wonderful place where he was needed.

Witnessing the slow disappearance of my friend, my husband, my lover, the father of my children was too much to bear. Throughout this journey, I had always described the disease as a giant eraser, slowly making Joe disappear from the pages of our lives. I realize now, after three years of him being with our Lord, he wasn't erased. The essence of who

Joe was before and during his illness remains with those who loved him.

I was the last member to join the "Storm Sisters" group. I know in my heart that it was God's plan for me to meet the ladies when I did. Being a Storm Sister provided me with the opportunity to share personal experiences and feelings that I couldn't normally share with others, unless they were widows or recovering caregivers like myself. It was a relief to know that in the loneliness, I wasn't alone. Our journeys, while different, brought us to a place of togetherness. It was okay to cry, laugh, reflect and feel supported. Having fellowship with these ladies made me feel special and filled my heart with joy. I felt a bond had been formed in the midst of our pain and suffering. Healing came with our gatherings. For this I am, and will always be, eternally grateful.

***

I too am extremely grateful for the women that opened their hearts to me and all that gathered during different times. We remain in contact with each other. Some of them get together on their own. When I shared with them that I was praying about retiring and leaving New York, they were very supportive and said we would plan trips together!

Yes, you read it correctly, I was praying about leaving New York. But, I must share why this decision came about. I was at my appointment with the orthopedic doctor who treated my knee. He showed me the current imaging and x-rays, and very little had changed with the osteoarthritis in my left knee. He sat down next to me and said, "I know you are a woman of great faith (I hope you pray for me) and I know you put that anointing oil on your knee, and you do the stretching, use the "Bio freeze". However, if you continue walking to work on the cement sidewalks, walk from the Palliative Care office to the hospital, walk all around the hospital and stand at your patient's bedside, I will need to do a knee replacement! Rosa, you are nearing retirement age, so please consider that. I feel, while you aren't at the stage of having a knee replacement surgery yet, slipping and sliding during this icy, snowy winter is affecting you!"

I spoke to my daughters, Ruth and Tirzah, and they agreed. But, I struggled leaving them and my grandchildren in New York. I asked my family, friends and church to pray for this decision. So, in 2018, I informed the Department of Family and Social Medicine and the Palliative Care Service that I was resigning my position of Palliative Care Chaplain, effective October 2018. WOW!

A verse my mother always shared with me helped in this next phase of life: Proverbs 3:5 & 6 (KJV), "Trust in the Lord with all thine heart; and lean not unto thine own understanding. In all thy ways acknowledge him, and he shall direct thy paths." So, I began downsizing, packing boxes, giving away things I wasn't taking, with the help of my daughters and friends. I was leaving the apartment we'd lived in for 24 years, the Norwood neighbor-hood where we had lived for 36 years and the borough of the Bronx, New York where I'd lived for 60-plus years!

As I told my neighbors, coworkers and friends my planned date of leaving, they would get sad and tell me "don't go." The hospital arranged a retirement party, while some of my former colleagues and current members of

Palliative Care Service arranged a separate more intimate time together. My pastor, Joseph Cortese, asked me to share a message of "Hope" with the church and then blessed me with a gift. I gave him a large bottle of Alpha & Omega anointing oil which made him very happy! My daughter, Tirzah, and dear friends, Carmen, Iliana, Eva, arranged a surprise party, along with my M&M friends (a nickname my husband Hermes gave them), Miriam and Myriam, who are DJ's.

The biggest transition came when I decided to return to live down South. My sister, Amy, and her husband, Jesus, arrived from Georgia and we drove back to their home, where I would stay for a few months. Then, I made the final move, driving to Florida to stay with my sister, Rachel, and her husband, Joe, until I was able to find a place to live. Talk about an adventurous transition!

My biggest surprise blessing came to me when Rachel and Joe sat with me and shared that they were purchasing another house, a home for me to rent and live in peacefully! Never did I see that coming. God is faithful in providing for the widow and the orphan. I remembered that 25 years earlier, the home (parsonage) where we lived was taken away, and now God restored my faith by blessing me with a home. It reminded me of the portion in Ruth 2:12 (ESV), "The Lord will repay you for what you have done, and a full reward be given you by the Lord, the God of Israel, under whose wings you have come to take refuge."

In this year of 2020, we are experiencing a worldwide coronavirus, COVID-19 pandemic, with more than 9 million cases in the U.S. and more than 38 million cases worldwide, as well as millions of deaths. We are sheltering in place, quarantining, social distancing, wearing masks, along with a mental health crisis of depression, fear and isolation. We've even had to relinquish our caregiving to hospital workers, say our final goodbyes to our loved ones on phone calls and mourn via skype or Facebook live streaming. A few months ago, when my dear friend Madeline, "Mady" as we affectionately called her, died in New York, it saddened me that I could not be at her funeral. I was grateful my daughter, Tirzah, was there with Mady's daughter, Jeanette, like Jeanette was with me when Hermes was dying in Florida.

We will continue to pray Psalm 91 over our loved ones and communities. Praying that Jehovah Rapha continues to provide healing to our bodies and souls. Thank you for joining me in this journey. I pray the Lord bless you, keep you and fill you with HOPE!

Psalm 33:22 (NLT) "Let your unfailing love surround us, Lord, for our hope is in you alone."

Resources

Alzheimer's Association - www.ALZ.org

Administration for Community Living - www.ACL.gov

AARP

Family Caregivers Alliance - www.caregiver.org

Five Wishes Advance Directives - www.fivewishes.org

Other Publications by Rosa Caraballo

- Caraballo, Rosa J. Covenant of Hope./ Pacto De Esperanza, Library of Congress Control Number:2004105173 ISBN: 0-9741927-7-5 Ebed Press July 2004

- Innovations at End-of-Life, Journal of Palliative Medicine, Palliative Care and HIV/AIDS at a Large Urban Teaching Hospital: Clinical Challenges and Program Description, Selwyn, Peter,

M.D., M.P.H. Rivard, Mimi, M.S., NP
Kappell, Deborah, M.P.H. Goeren, Bill,
M.S.W. La Fosse, Hector, AA Schwartz,
Charles, M.D. Rev. Rosa Caraballo,
Luciano, Delma, Farber Post, Linda,
2002

. The Sister Fund Special Report.
Spiritual Quest, The Struggle for Justice,
Spirituality and Justice: A Dialogue,
Caraballo, Rosa J. and various authors.